Bond
No.1 for exam success

CW00738505

Skills

Spelling and Vocabulary

9–10 years

OXFORD
UNIVERSITY PRESS

Great Clarendon Street, Oxford, OX2 6DP, United Kingdom

Oxford University Press is a department of the University of Oxford. It furthers the University's objective of excellence in research, scholarship, and education by publishing worldwide. Oxford is a registered trade mark of Oxford University Press in the UK and in certain other countries

Text © Michellejoy Hughes 2015

Illustrations © Oxford University Press 2015

The moral rights of the author have been asserted

First published in 2015

All rights reserved. No part of this publication may be reproduced, stored in a retrieval system, or transmitted, in any form or by any means, without the prior permission in writing of Oxford University Press, or as expressly permitted by law, by licence or under terms agreed with the appropriate reprographics rights organization. Enquiries concerning reproduction outside the scope of the above should be sent to the Rights Department, Oxford University Press, at the address above.

You must not circulate this work in any other form and you must impose this same condition on any acquirer

British Library Cataloguing in Publication Data
Data available

978-0-1927-9378-2
10 9 8 7 6 5 4 3 2 1

Paper used in the production of this book is a natural, recyclable product made from wood grown in sustainable forests. The manufacturing process conforms to the environmental regulations of the country of origin.

Printed in China

Acknowledgements

Cover illustrations: Lo Cole

Although we have made every effort to trace and contact all copyright holders before publication this has not been possible in all cases. If notified, the publisher will rectify any errors or omissions at the earliest opportunity.

Links to third party websites are provided by Oxford in good faith and for information only. Oxford disclaims any responsibility for the materials contained in any third party website referenced in this work.

Unit 1

A All of the words are hidden in the word search. Once you have found all of the words, the remaining letters spell out a message that is related to your words. [17]

1 What is this message? _____

W	C	D	I	S	E	A	S	E	H
O	H	E	X	C	E	E	D	A	E
B	E	A	K	E	R	R	D	G	A
E	A	T	H	R	E	A	T	L	L
A	P	H	E	A	V	E	N	E	T
K	F	E	A	T	H	E	R	W	H
G	L	E	A	M	I	N	G	H	Y
H	E	A	T	H	E	R	S	E	W
S	P	E	A	K	E	R	I	A	T
H	W	E	A	K	E	N	E	T	A

B Some of these words can have one letter removed and they will make a new word. Can you remove one letter from these words and write the new word that can be made? [8]

1 Beaker _____ **5** Cheap _____

2 Feather _____ **6** Healthy _____

3 Heaven _____ **7** Wheat _____

4 Weaken _____ **8** Threat _____

Beak

Beaker

Cheap

Death

Disease

Eagle

Exceed

Feather

Gleaming

Healthy

Heather

Heaven

Speaker

Threat

Weaken

Wheat

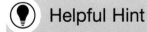 **Helpful Hint**

When we have double vowels a quick reminder to help us spell is: *When two vowels go out walking, the first sound does the talking.* So 'ea' often sounds like 'E'.

/ 25

Unit 1

Art

Ban

Bud

Cob

Con

Dot

Dye

Fee

Gap

Gum

Hum

Ivy

Shy

Sty

Tin

Wry

C Which of the three letter words in your list can be found in these longer words? [16]

1   Dehumanise   _____

2   Martyrs   _____

3   Anecdotal   _____

4   Budgerigar   _____

5   Polystyrene   _____

6   Coffeepot   _____

7   Archdeacons   _____

8   Privy   _____

9   Delighting   _____

10   Argument   _____

11   Dowry   _____

12   Midyear   _____

13   Turban   _____

14   Cobwebs   _____

15   Megaphone   _____

16   Squashy   _____

D Place one of the following words in each space below using all of the words once: [10]

| art   ban   bud   con   fee   gap   hum   sty   tin   wry |

1–2   To which two words can we add an 'a' to make another word?

_____ and _____

3–4   To which two words can we add a 'p' to make another word?

_____ and _____

5–6   To which two words can we add an 'e' to make another word?

_____ and _____

7–8   To which two words can we add a 't' to make another word?

_____ and _____

9–10   To which two words can we add an 's' to make another word?

_____ and _____

26

Unit 1

E All of the words are hidden in the word search. Once you have found all of the words, the remaining letters spell out a message that is related to your words. [17]

1 What is this message? _____

N	S	T	R	E	N	G	T	H
I	T	H	F	E	T	C	H	E
N	S	E	B	A	T	H	W	O
T	R	P	I	D	D	U	L	W
H	H	I	R	S	E	R	A	E
B	U	N	C	H	P	C	T	A
M	N	C	H	A	T	H	C	L
O	C	H	L	L	H	U	H	T
T	H	U	T	C	H	S	E	H
H	L	E	N	G	T	H	T	H
O	R	C	W	I	D	T	H	H

F An antonym is a word that is most opposite in meaning to another. Which of your words are antonyms for these words? [3]

1 Take _____

2 Weakness _____

3 Poverty _____

G A synonym is a word that is similar in meaning to another. Which of your words are synonyms for these words? [4]

1 Nip _____

2 Clump _____

3 Power _____

4 Cage _____

Bath

Birch

Bunch

Church

Depth

Fetch

Hunch

Hutch

Latch

Length

Moth

Ninth

Pinch

Strength

Wealth

Width

24

Bond Skills Spelling and Vocabulary 9–10

Ape

Bore

Cave

Cove

Drake

Fate

Frame

Kite

Lace

Rake

Rate

Spoke

Tape

Tone

Tune

Wove

22

(H) Place one of the words in each space so that each sentence makes sense. [16]

1 _____ is an intricate pattern or decorative fabric.

2 Another word for ribbon is _____ .

3 A songwriter sets words to a _____ .

4 Around the coast we find a _____ which is a sheltered bay.

5 An _____ is an animal.

6 _____ means luck or fortune.

7 A border around a photograph or picture is called a _____ .

8 The past tense of speak is _____ .

9 The _____ is the cost or speed of something.

10 A _____ is a hollow or tunnel in a cliff, hill or mountainside.

11 On a windy day it is great fun to fly a _____ .

12 To _____ is to drill a hole.

13 The past tense of weave is _____ .

14 The word _____ means a shade, or a musical sound, or to shape up.

15 A male duck is called a _____ .

16 A _____ is a gardening tool.

(I) All of these words have an 'e' at the end, but some of these words would make another word if we took the 'e' off. Find six words that would make another word if the 'e' was removed. [6]

1 _____   4 _____

2 _____   5 _____

3 _____   6 _____

Recap   6

Unit 2

(A) All of the words are hidden in the word search. Once you have found all of the words, the remaining letters spell out a message that is related to your words. [17]

1　What is this message? _____

G	B	A	N	A	N	A	W	O	S
R	A	S	P	B	E	R	R	Y	T
A	P	R	I	C	O	T	R	P	R
P	I	N	E	A	P	P	L	E	A
E	D	S	T	O	H	A	E	A	W
F	C	H	E	R	R	Y	M	C	B
R	H	U	B	A	R	B	O	H	E
U	T	A	R	N	E	F	N	R	R
I	M	A	N	G	O	U	I	T	R
T	L	I	M	E	P	L	U	M	Y
A	P	P	L	E	G	R	A	P	E

(B) Can you spell the following words backwards and then put these new words into alphabetical order? [10]

grape	cherry	lemon	mango	peach

_____　_____　_____　_____　_____

1st _____　2nd _____　3rd _____　4th _____　5th _____

 Helpful Hint

Some fruits make use of common spelling strings. If you can spell 'cherry' you can spell all of the 'berry' words (cranberry, strawberry, blueberry, etc.) and the plural of this 'cherries' gives you the same spelling string as all of the plural 'berries'.

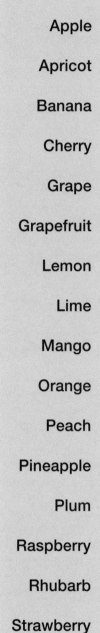

Apple

Apricot

Banana

Cherry

Grape

Grapefruit

Lemon

Lime

Mango

Orange

Peach

Pineapple

Plum

Raspberry

Rhubarb

Strawberry

27

Unit 2

Acorn

Armour

Bandage

Bandit

Bargain

Bathe

Birthday

Bitten

Blackbird

Bluebell

Buttercup

Butterflies

Cupcake

Damage

Daydream

Download

16

(c) Can you use the words in your spelling list and the clues below to complete this crossword? [16]

Across

1 To physically harm
3 A knight's protective clothing
5 Pretty insects
7 A garden bird
10 A tasty treat
11 To be gnawed
12 To go into a trance
13 To celebrate our age

Down

1 To get online information
2 A wild flower
3 The fruit of an oak tree
4 To buy something cheaply
6 To soak
7 A spring flower
8 Found in a first aid kit
9 A thief or robber

 Helpful Hint

All compound words have to be made from two, or more, proper words so think about this to help you with your spellings, especially when they do not sound like their component words.

D All the words in your list are in the grid but only the first letters are here. Can you fill in the gaps so that the grid is complete? [16]

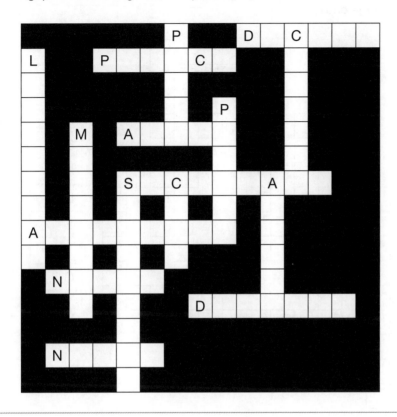

Actor

Architect

Artist

Chef

Curator

Dentist

Doctor

Librarian

Musician

Nanny

Nurse

Pilot

Police

Priest

Scientist

Secretary

E Which of these words fit the descriptions below? [8]

1 Who works with play scripts? __ __ __ __ __

2 Who flies an aeroplane? __ __ __ __ __

3 Who looks after children? __ __ __ __ __

4 Who works with paint? __ __ __ __ __ __

5 Who works in an office? __ __ __ __ __ __ __ __ __

6 Who creates meals? __ __ __ __

7 Who looks after our teeth? __ __ __ __ __ __ __

8 Who designs buildings? __ __ __ __ __ __ __ __ __

24

Unit 2

Amuse

Bike

Blade

Blame

Complete

Crime

Describe

Dome

Entire

File

Flame

Flute

Glide

Globe

Primrose

Strange

F) All of the words in your list are in the grid but the letters have been replaced by numbers. Can you work out which number represents which letter so that you can fill in the grid? [18]

	4		6	
26	5	25	7	13

(crossword grid with numbers)

A			L	
B			M	
C			N	
D			O	
E			P	
F			R	
G			S	
I			T	
K			U	

G) A synonym is a word that is most similar in meaning to another word. Which of your words are synonyms for these words? [10]

1   Entertain   _____

2   Slide   _____

3   Offence   _____

4   Document   _____

5   Eerie   _____

6   Accuse   _____

7   Finish   _____

8   Whole   _____

9   Earth   _____

10   Blaze   _____

28

Unit 3

A All of your words are in the grid, but the letters have been replaced with numbers. Can you work out which number represents each letter to solve the puzzle? [20]

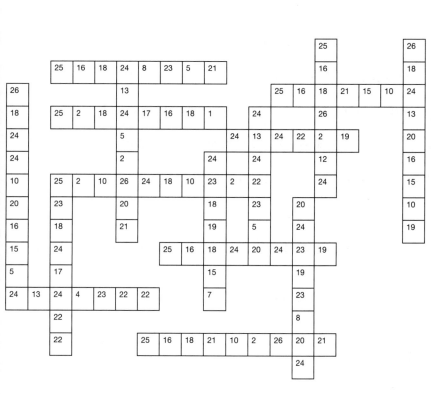

A	
B	
C	
D	
E	24
F	
G	
H	
I	
K	
L	
M	
N	
O	
R	
S	
T	
U	
V	
W	
Y	

Eardrum

Eyeball

Eyelash

Eyelid

Eyesight

Farewell

Fingernail

Firework

Forecast

Forehead

Forgive

Fortnight

Fortune

Greenhouse

Greyhound

Headache

B Can you divide the 4 words below from your list into their two component words? [4]

_____Ear_____ + _____Drum_____ = _____Eardrum_____

1 _____+_____ = Forecast

2 _____+_____ = Forgive

3 _____+_____ = Greyhound

4 _____+_____ = Headache

24

Unit 3

Believe

Brief

Ceiling

Chief

Deceive

Eerie

Eighth

Either

Experience

Mischief

Niece

Pierce

Receipt

Relieved

Replied

Weird

16

ⓒ Place one of your words into each space so that each sentence makes sense. [16]

1   Camping was a brilliant _____ as we were so close to nature.

2   My auntie says that I am her favourite _____ .

3   It was so _____ seeing my teacher on holiday in the same hotel!

4   The woods at night became an _____ place to be.

5   The kitten caused _____ by unravelling the ball of wool.

6   The _____ engineer was in charge of five other engineers.

7   I returned the broken crockery to the shop as I had the _____ .

8   I do _____ that reading books widens our vocabulary.

9   The pupils were asked to answer _____ question one or question two.

10 Nobody _____ when we knocked on the door.

11 The boy tried to _____ the teacher, but the teacher had the results.

12 Unfortunately, out of eight pupils, the boy came _____ .

13 We all took a _____ break before returning to the meeting room.

14 The decorator painted the _____ to lighten the room.

15 I was _____ when I had my results and knew that my leg wasn't broken.

16 You might _____ the balloon if you put it near the rose bush.

💡 Helpful Hint

The famous reminder for spelling 'ie' and 'ei' words is: I before E except after C but some WEIRD words are DISAGREEING so don't forget EITHER or NEITHER!

Unit 3

D Use a line to join up the animals with the name used for its baby. [16]

| cow | deer | dog | duck | ferret | fish | fox | frog |

calf		chick		cub	cygnet	duckling
fawn		foal	fry	gosling	kid	kit
lamb		owlet		piglet	puppy	tadpole

| goat | goose | hen | horse | pig | owl | sheep | swan |

E Can you spell the following words backwards and then put these new words into alphabetical order? [8]

| owlet | piglet | cygnet | kit |

_____ _____ _____ _____

1st _____   2nd _____   3rd _____   4th _____

Calf

Chick

Cub

Cygnet

Duckling

Fawn

Foal

Fry

Gosling

Kid

Kit

Lamb

Owlet

Piglet

Puppy

Tadpole

Helpful Hint

The ending 'let' is used for many words to show they are diminutive or small.
Can you think of other words that end in 'let' that follow this pattern?

24

Unit 3

Admit

Adult

Alert

Fight

Float

Garnet

Grant

Habit

Habitat

Inspect

Instant

Instruct

Insult

Reject

Sprint

Toilet

(F) All of these words are in the word search. Once you have found them all, the left-over letters spell out a message that is related to your words. [17]

1   What is this message? _____

H	A	B	I	T	A	T	T	I	F
A	D	M	I	T	D	H	G	N	I
B	E	S	E	A	U	L	A	S	G
I	L	E	N	A	L	E	R	T	H
T	O	I	L	E	T	D	N	A	T
G	I	N	S	U	L	T	E	N	F
R	I	N	S	P	E	C	T	T	L
A	I	N	S	T	R	U	C	T	O
N	R	E	J	E	C	T	I	N	A
T	S	P	R	I	N	T	A	T	T

(G) An antonym is a word that has an opposite meaning to another word. Which of your words are antonyms for these words? [6]

1   Sink   _____   4   Praise   _____

2   Deny   _____   5   Sleepy   _____

3   Accept   _____   6   Child   _____

23

Recap   14

Unit 4

(A) Can you use the clues below to complete the crossword? All of the answers are in your word list. [16]

Across

2 One person
3 A game played on horseback
4 Information
5 A large country
7 Seating for more than one person
10 Two people
11 A sound that repeats
12 A place that shows films
14 Baggage
15 Region

Down

1 A vegetable
2 Fizzy water
6 Three people
8 A tiny fly
9 A chocolate drink
13 A period of time

Area

Cargo

China

Cinema

Cocoa

Data

Duo

Echo

Era

Flea

Polo

Potato

Soda

Sofa

Solo

Trio

 Helpful Hint

The vowel that is most commonly used to end English words is an 'e'. Words from other languages end in other vowels. Can you find out where your words originate from?

16

Unit 4

Bride

Bridle

Eight

Faction

Fraction

Haze

Hazel

Height

Learn

Learnt

Print

Reign

Rein

Sprint

Vanish

Varnish

16

(B) If we added one letter to half of the words in your list, we would make the words from the other half. Can you place the correct word in the space so that these sentences make sense? [16]

1   We have a _____ tree in our garden.

2   A _____ is the long strap attached to the horse's bit.

3   I completed my homework but did not get chance to _____ it out.

4   Soaking the material in bleach made the stain _____ overnight.

5   The _____ path was used by many horses.

6   I need to _____ my multiplication tables for a test next week.

7   There were _____ children in the group.

8   A quarter is a _____ meaning one out of four.

9   The runner managed to _____ for the last part of the race.

10 I have _____ how to ride my bike without stabilisers.

11 The _____ and groom were married last week.

12 The islands could just be seen below the _____ of cloud and sunlight.

13 One splinter group, or _____ , joined the debate with an alternate view.

14 Queen Victoria's _____ was between 1837 and 1901.

15 If we _____ the wood it will be much more durable.

16 The _____ of the tree was perfect for nesting owls.

 Helpful Hint

Can you think of other pairs of words where the first word can have a letter added to make another word? You might be surprised how many you can find!

(c) All the words in your list are in the grid but only the first letters are here. Can you fill in the gaps so that the grid is complete? [16]

(d) These words all have double consonants in them. If we break each word into syllables, the break will fall between the two double letters: 'an-noyed'. This is a good way of remembering how to spell them. Can you split 14 of the words into their syllables, remembering to split the double letters in the middle? [14]

1 _____

2 _____

3 _____

4 _____

5 _____

6 _____

7 _____

8 _____

9 _____

10 _____

11 _____

12 _____

13 _____

14 _____

Announce

Annoyed

Attend

Banner

Bitter

Burrow

Butter

Cotton

Cuddle

Effect

Fluffy

Followed

Kettle

Summer

Teddies

Village

30

Unit 4

Caught

Court

Currant

Current

Guessed

Guest

Heard

Herd

Idle

Idol

Morning

Mourning

Stationary

Stationery

Vain

Vein

20

(E) A homophone is a word that sounds like another but has a different spelling and a different meaning. These words are all homophones. Can you draw a line to join the word to its correct definition? [16]

1	Caught	Carries our blood along.
2	Court	Between midnight and noon.
3	Currant	Someone invited into your home.
4	Current	Where a judge considers evidence.
5	Guessed	To be lazy.
6	Guest	The past tense of catch.
7	Heard	Paper, envelopes, pens and pencils.
8	Herd	The past tense of hear.
9	Idle	A dried grape.
10	Idol	To be bereaved after a death or loss.
11	Morning	An electrical flow.
12	Mourning	Formed an answer without knowledge.
13	Stationary	A group of animals such as cows.
14	Stationery	To feel overly proud of appearance.
15	Vain	Not moving.
16	Vein	An object that is worshipped.

(F) An antonym is a word that is most opposite in meaning to another word. Which of your words is an antonym for these words? [4]

| 1 | Afternoon | _____ | 3 | Moving | _____ |
| 2 | Busy | _____ | 4 | Modest | _____ |

(A) Can you add twelve of your spellings to this grid so that it is complete? One letter in each word has been provided as a clue. [12]

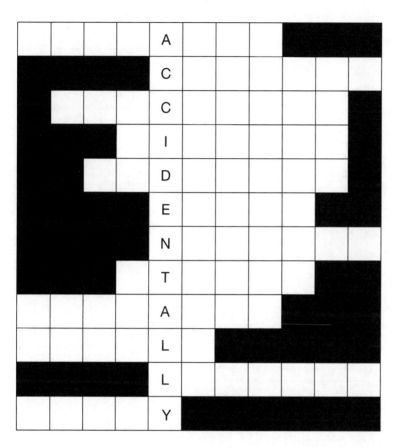

(B) A synonym is a word whose meaning is most similar to another. Which of your words are synonyms for the following words? [4]

1 Really _____

2 Normal _____

3 Sometimes _____

4 Likely _____

Accidentally

Actually

Beady

Bubbly

Century

Essay

Ferry

History

Injury

Library

Naughty

Occasionally

Ordinary

Probably

Specially

Sturdy

💡 Helpful Hint

A common spelling rule for adding a 'y' at the end of some words is this:
If a word ends in an 'e' that you cannot hear, drop the 'e' and add the 'y'.
So bubble = bubbly, injure = injury.

16

Unit 5

Black

Blue

Brown

Gold

Green

Grey

Indigo

Navy

Pink

Purple

Scarlet

Silver

Tan

Turquoise

White

Yellow

Ⓒ All of the words in your list are here in this word search. Once you have found them all, the left-over letters spell out a message that is related to these words. [17]

1 What is this message? _____

G	O	L	D	C	O	B	L	U	E
L	P	U	R	P	L	E	O	G	Y
U	R	F	S	I	L	V	E	R	E
G	R	E	E	N	U	L	T	E	L
B	L	A	C	K	W	O	A	Y	L
R	I	N	D	I	G	O	N	R	O
O	S	C	A	R	L	E	T	D	W
W	H	I	T	E	S	N	A	V	Y
N	T	U	R	Q	U	O	I	S	E

Ⓓ Can you write the following words backwards and then place these new words into alphabetical order: [10]

black   brown   green   pink   tan

_____ _____ _____ _____ _____

1st _____ 2nd _____ 3rd _____ 4th _____ 5th _____

💡 **Helpful Hint**

Now you have some excellent descriptive words, make sure you use them. Leave 'red' and 'blue' and describe your character as wearing a **scarlet** dress, describe the sea as **turquoise** with flashes of **navy**. Why not find more descriptive colours to help your writing even more?

27

(E) All of these words have more than one meaning, which means they are homonyms. Which one word fits both definitions in these questions? [16]

1   A fried sliver of potato. Cool.   _____

2   Curiosity. The additional sum awarded for saving money.   _____

3   A mathematical shape. A percussion musical instrument.   _____

4   Left over remains of a fire. A tree.   _____

5   A stand alone clause. A term of punishment.   _____

6   To rip. The product created when we cry.   _____

7   A narrow boat. To shove or push.   _____

8   A burgundy, red colour. To abandon.   _____

9   Where we live. To give a lecture or talk.   _____

10 A sharp point. To move very quickly.   _____

11 A container for petrol or water. A vehicle used by the army. _____

12 To badly miss somebody or something. An evergreen tree. _____

13 A bird. To move with great speed.   _____

14 A sticky, dried fruit. Part of a calendar.   _____

15 A gemstone. A shape.   _____

16 To tap repeatedly. A percussion musical instrument.   _____

| Address |
| Ash |
| Barge |
| Crisp |
| Dart |
| Date |
| Diamond |
| Drum |
| Interest |
| Maroon |
| Pine |
| Sentence |
| Swift |
| Tank |
| Tear |
| Triangle |

Helpful Hint

These homonyms can be tricky, but a lot of the time a homonym is a verb and a noun. Think of 'water': I can get a drink of water or I can water my plants. Always ask yourself if the word is an action, a thing or both.

16

Unit 5

Connect

Flutter

Hurry

Pillow

Rattle

Ribbon

Rotten

Ruffle

Shatter

Shopper

Shopping

Shutter

Silly

Spotty

Stripped

Summit

(F) Find the words that fit the definitions below. [16]

1   Someone who buys things.   _____

2   Stale or mouldy.   _____

3   Daft or foolish.   _____

4   Made bare.   _____

5   To go quickly.   _____

6   Purchasing items.   _____

7   The movement of butterfly wings.   _____

8   To shake.   _____

9   A wooden window closure.   _____

10 To have blotches.   _____

11 A cushion for the bed.   _____

12 To join together.   _____

13 A colourful tape.   _____

14 To smash into pieces.   _____

15 A decorative piece of fabric.   _____

16 The top of a mountain.   _____

16

(↻) Recap

Answers

Unit 1

Ⓐ 1 Secret message: WORDS WITH EA

Ⓑ 1 Baker 5 Heap / Chap
2 Father 6 Health
3 Haven / Heave 7 Heat / What / Whet
4 Waken 8 Treat

Ⓒ 1 Hum 5 Sty 9 Tin 13 Ban
2 Art 6 Fee 10 Gum 14 Cob
3 Dot 7 Con 11 Wry 15 Gap
4 Bud 8 Ivy 12 Dye 16 Shy

Ⓓ 1–2 Stay, Wary
3–4 Part, Hump
5–6 Any two of the following: Bean, Bane, Cone, Gape, Tine, Stye
7–8 Any two of the following: Tart, Feet, Tint
9–10 Any two of the following: Arts, Bans, Buds, Cons, Fees, Gaps, Hums

Ⓔ 1 Secret message: THESE WORDS ALL USE TH OR CH

Ⓕ 1 Fetch 3 Wealth
2 Strength

Ⓖ 1 Pinch 3 Strength
2 Bunch 4 Hutch

Ⓗ 1 Lace 5 Ape 9 Rate 13 Wove
2 Tape 6 Fate 10 Cave 14 Tone
3 Tune 7 Frame 11 Kite 15 Drake
4 Cove 8 Spoke 12 Bore 16 Rake

Ⓘ In any order:
1 Fate (fat) 4 Tape (tap)
2 Kite (kit) 5 Tone (ton)
3 Rate (rat) 6 Tune (tun)

Unit 2

Ⓐ 1 Secret message: WORDS THAT ARE FRUIT

Ⓑ 1st Eparg 4th Ognam
2nd Hcaep 5th Yrrehc
3rd Nomel

Ⓒ Across: Down:
1 Damage 1 Download
3 Armour 2 Buttercup
5 Butterflies 3 Acorn
7 Blackbird 4 Bargain
10 Cupcake 6 Bathe
11 Bitten 7 Bluebell
12 Daydream 8 Bandage
13 Birthday 9 Bandit

Ⓓ

Ⓔ 1 Actor 5 Secretary
2 Pilot 6 Chef
3 Nanny 7 Dentist
4 Artist 8 Architect

Ⓕ

17	4	26	6	13	12	21	25	22	1	7	18	16	9	5	19	3	10
A	B	C	D	E	F	G	I	K	L	M	N	O	P	R	S	T	U

Ⓖ 1 Amuse 6 Blame
2 Glide 7 Complete
3 Crime 8 Entire
4 File 9 Globe
5 Strange 10 Flame

Unit 3

Ⓐ

23	4	8	19	24	25	26	20	2	1	22	7	10	16	18	5	21	15	12	17	13
A	B	C	D	E	F	G	H	I	K	L	M	N	O	R	S	T	U	V	W	Y

Ⓑ 1 Fore + Cast = Forecast
2 For + Give = Forgive
3 Grey + Hound = Greyhound
4 Head + Ache = Headache

Ⓒ 1 Experience 9 Either
2 Niece 10 Replied
3 Weird 11 Deceive
4 Eerie 12 Eighth
5 Mischief 13 Brief
6 Chief 14 Ceiling
7 Receipt 15 Relieved
8 Believe 16 Pierce

Ⓓ In any order:
1 Cow = Calf 9 Goat = Kid
2 Deer = Fawn 10 Goose = Gosling
3 Dog = Puppy 11 Hen = Chick
4 Duck = Duckling 12 Horse = Foal
5 Ferret = Kit 13 Pig = Piglet
6 Fish = Fry 14 Owl = Owlet
7 Fox = Cub 15 Sheep = Lamb
8 Frog = Tadpole 16 Swan = Cygnet

Ⓔ 1st Telgip 3rd Tengyc
2nd Telwo 4th Tik

Ⓕ 1 Secret message: THESE ALL END IN A T

Ⓖ 1 Float 4 Insult
2 Admit 5 Alert
3 Reject 6 Adult

ANSWERS

Unit 4

Ⓐ **Across:**
2 Solo
3 Polo
4 Data
5 China
7 Sofa
10 Duo
11 Echo
12 Cinema
14 Cargo
15 Area

Down:
1 Potato
2 Soda
6 Trio
8 Flea
9 Cocoa
13 Era

Ⓑ
1 Hazel
2 Rein
3 Print
4 Vanish
5 Bridle
6 Learn
7 Eight
8 Fraction
9 Sprint
10 Learnt
11 Bride
12 Haze
13 Faction
14 Reign
15 Varnish
16 Height

Ⓒ

Note: BUTTER and BITTER could also be placed the other way around.

Ⓓ **Any 14 of the following:**
1 At-tend
2 Ban-ner
3 Bit-ter
4 Bur-row
5 But-ter
6 Cot-ton
7 Cud-dle
8 Ef-fect
9 Fluf-fy
10 Fol-lowed
11 Ket-tle
12 Sum-mer
13 Vil-lage
14 Ted-dies
15 An-nounce

Ⓔ
1 Caught = The past tense of catch
2 Court = Where a judge considers evidence
3 Currant = A dried grape
4 Current = An electrical flow
5 Guessed = Formed an answer without knowledge
6 Guest = Someone invited into your home
7 Heard = The past tense of hear
8 Herd = A group of animals such as cows
9 Idle = To be lazy
10 Idol = An object that is worshipped
11 Morning = Between midnight and noon
12 Mourning = To be bereaved after a death or loss
13 Stationary = Not moving
14 Stationery = Paper, envelopes, pens and pencils
15 Vain = To feel overly proud of appearance
16 Vein = Carries along our blood

Ⓕ
1 Morning
2 Idle
3 Stationary
4 Vain

Unit 5

Ⓐ

PROBABLY
CENTURY
SPECIALLY
HISTORY
ORDINARY
ESSAY
NAUGHTY
STURDY
ACTUALLY
BUBBLY
LIBRARY
BEADY

Ⓑ
1 Actually
2 Ordinary
3 Occasionally
4 Probably

Ⓒ 1 **Secret message:** COLOURFUL WORDS

Ⓓ
1st Kcalb
2nd Knip
3rd Nat
4th Neerg
5th Nworb

Ⓔ
1 Crisp
2 Interest
3 Triangle
4 Ash
5 Sentence
6 Tear
7 Barge
8 Maroon
9 Address
10 Dart
11 Tank
12 Pine
13 Swift
14 Date
15 Diamond
16 Drum

Ⓕ
1 Shopper
2 Rotten
3 Silly
4 Stripped
5 Hurry
6 Shopping
7 Flutter
8 Rattle
9 Shutter
10 Spotty
11 Pillow
12 Connect
13 Ribbon
14 Shatter
15 Ruffle
16 Summit

Unit 6

Ⓐ
1 Sun + flower
2 Sun + light
3 Sun + shine
4 Sup + ply
5 Sup + port
6 Tab + let
7 Tar + get
8 Tea + cup
9 Tea + pot
10 Tea + spoon
11 Thin + king
12 Toad + stool
13 Toe + nail
14 Trap + door
15 Tea + time

Ⓑ
1 Door 2 Sheet 3 Brood 4 Feel

Ⓒ
1 C e k o o r
2 G l m o o y
3 E e g r t
4 E e e l s v
5 F h i l o o s

Ⓓ
1st Moorb
2nd Neek
3rd Pooc
4th Pool
5th Sroodni

(E) **In any order:**

1	Snowball	9	Password
2	Moonlight	10	Railway
3	Passport	11	Overall
4	Outlaw	12	Raincoat
5	Rainbow	13	Snowdrop
6	Outstanding	14	Overtake
7	Overheard	15	Snowflake
8	Package	16	Outside

(F) **Prepositions:**
Outstanding, Overheard, Overall, Overtake, Outside
Nature: Snowball, Rainbow, Raincoat,

Snowdrop, Snowflake
Other: Passport, Railway, Password

(G)
1	Possession	6	Argue
2	Business	7	Especially
3	Particular	8	Peculiar
4	Guide	9	Thought
5	Separate	10	Definite

(H)

Unit 7

(A)

(B)
1	Disappear	3	Dusk
2	Dawn	4	Impossible

(C)

Note: STEEP and SHEET could also be placed the other way around.

(D) **In any order:**
1 **'OO'** sound: smooth, spoon,
2 **'E'** sound: meeting, needle, queen, sheet, steep, teeth, weekend, creepy, freezing
3 **Not 'OO' or 'E'** sound: moor, wooden, loose

(E)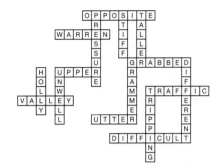

Note: UPPER and UTTER could also be placed the other way around.

(F)
1	Difficult	3	Upper
2	Grabbed	4	Taller

(G)
1	Reduction	9	Division
2	Portion	10	Position
3	Decision	11	Television
4	Creation	12	Collection
5	Mention	13	Version
6	Rejection	14	Option
7	Addition	15	Caution
8	Multiplication	16	Question

Unit 8

(A)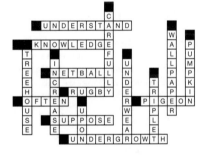

(B) **Any six of the following:**
Know + Ledge = Knowledge
Net + Ball = Netball
Of + Ten = Often
Pig + Eon = Pigeon
Pump + Kin = Pumpkin
Rug + By = Rugby
Sup + Pose = Suppose
Tree + House = Treehouse
Trip + Let = Triplet
Under + Growth = Undergrowth
Under + Stand = Understand
Under + Wear = Underwear
Up + On = Upon
Wall + Paper = Wallpaper
Care + Fully = Carefully

(C)

17	5	14	10	12	15	11	2	26	22	16	20	4	13	25	24	23	6	8
A	B	C	D	E	F	G	H	I	K	L	N	O	P	R	S	T	U	W

(D)
1–3	Double 'S': Chess, Glass, Guess
4–8	Double 'L': Retell, Shrill, Skull, Stallion, Telling
9	Double 'F': Giraffe

ANSWERS

10 Double 'E': Cheese
11–12 Double 'R': Corridor, Sparrow
13–14 Double 'T': Knitting, Lettuce
15 Double 'B': Rabbit

(E) **1 Message:** GAMES AND SPORT VOCABULARY

(F) **Ball Games:** Baseball, Basketball, Cricket, Golf, Hockey, Rounders, Snooker, Squash, Tennis
No Ball Games: Judo, Jumping, Riding, Running, Swimming, Athletics, Badminton (Although Badminton is a racquet sport it uses a shuttlecock instead of a ball).

(H) Accept any 10 correctly spelt words using these letters.
For example: am, as, clump, clumps, cup, cups, cusp, map, maps, maul, mauls, plum, plums, seal, seam, spam, sup, up

Unit 9

(A) **Across:**
2 Trumpet
5 Spider
7 Sting
8 Shirt
9 Skirt
10 Smack
11 Gloves

Down:
1 Flesh
2 Thump
3 Chin
4 Writing
6 Drink
7 Spine
8 Scarf
9 Shove
12 Swan

(B) **1** Cause = The opposite of 'effect'.
2 Cheek = Part of our face.
3 Curtain = A fabric covering for a window.
4 Dairy = Milk, cheese, cream and yoghurt food types.
5 Diary = A little book with days and dates in it.
6 Diet = The food and drink that we eat.
7 Fairy = A little mythical creature with wings.
8 Fiery = Very hot.
9 Flavour = The taste of something.
10 Fruit = Apple, orange, pear and cherry food types.
11 Goose = A large bird.
12 Lion = An animal that roars and lives in groups called 'prides'.
13 Mainly = Mostly.
14 Piano = A percussion musical instrument with a keyboard.
15 Saint = A person who has lived an especially religious life.
16 Toast = Grilled bread.

(C) **1 Secret message:** ALL OF THESE WORDS END WITH AL

(D) **1** Petal
2 Annual
3 Canal
4 Hospital

(E) **1** Trousers
2 Brought
3 Curious
4 Youngest
5 Ought
6 Various
7 Countries
8 Would
9 Lounge
10 Course
11 Count
12 Group
13 Fought
14 Famous
15 Pounce
16 Should

Unit 10

(A)

(B) **1** Mount
2 Bun/Urn
3 Chat
4 Mean/Meat

(C) **1st** Tnatsid
2nd Tneced
3rd Tnecer
4th Tnedor
5th Tnetnoc

(D) **Across:**
2 Wagon
5 Woman
6 Certain
7 Potion
9 Women
10 Sudden
13 Robin
14 Chicken

Down:
1 Bacon
3 Guardian
4 Onion
5 Woken
8 Salmon
9 Widen
11 Urban
12 Grain

(E)

20	6	16	13	8	21	10	14	22	5	15	19	18	11	25	23	4	1	7	9
A	C	D	E	F	G	I	K	L	M	N	O	P	R	S	T	U	V	W	Z

(F) **1** Rifles
2 Roses
3 Slices
4 Surfaces
5 Knives
6 Vines
7 Sales
8 States

(G) **1** Calendar = An organiser of months and dates.
2 Cellar = An underground storage room.
3 Consider = To think about.
4 Farmer = Someone who looks after cows, pigs and sheep.
5 Finger = A digit on our hands.
6 Guitar = A stringed musical instrument.
7 Manager = Someone in charge.
8 Quartet = A group of four.
9 Remember = To not forget.
10 Similar = To be alike.
11 Sugar = A sweet additive.
12 Sweater = A jumper.
13 Teacher = Someone who gives an education to pupils.
14 Teenager = Someone between 13 and 19 years old.
15 Unclear = Confused.
16 Vicar = Someone who leads a church congregation.

Unit 6

(A) All of the words in your list are compound words. This means that each word is made from two other words. Can you divide your words into their two separate words? The first one is done for you as an example. [15]

Example: Sunbeam = _____*sun*_____ and _____*beam*_____

1   Sunflower = _____ and _____

2   Sunlight   = _____ and _____

3   Sunshine = _____ and _____

4   Supply   = _____ and _____

5   Support   = _____ and _____

6   Tablet   = _____ and _____

7   Target   = _____ and _____

8   Teacup   = _____ and _____

9   Teapot   = _____ and _____

10 Teaspoon = _____ and _____

11 Thinking = _____ and _____

12 Toadstool = _____ and _____

13 Toenail   = _____ and _____

14 Trapdoor = _____ and _____

15 Teatime   = _____ and _____

| Sunbeam |
| Sunflower |
| Sunlight |
| Sunshine |
| Supply |
| Support |
| Tablet |
| Target |
| Teacup |
| Teapot |
| Teaspoon |
| Teatime |
| Thinking |
| Toadstool |
| Toenail |
| Trapdoor |

💡 **Helpful Hint**

Now you have split up your words, have a go at mixing them up to create some new compound words. For example the word 'tea' could make 'teabag' and 'spoon' could make 'tablespoon'.

15

Unit 6

Blood

Breed

Broom

Cooker

Coop

Deer

Fleece

Fool

Foolish

Gloomy

Greet

Indoors

Keen

Loop

Sleeve

Shoot

19

(B) These words all have double 'e' or double 'o' in them, but some of these words make another word if the double vowels are swapped over. The first one is already done as an example, can you complete the others? [4]

_____Blood_____ = _____Bleed_____

1   Deer   = _____   3   Breed   = _____

2   Shoot = _____   4   Fool   = _____

(C) Can you put the letters of the following words in alphabetical order? The first one has already been done as an example. [5]

_____Fleece_____ = _c e e e f l_   3   Greet   = _____

1   Cooker = _____   4   Sleeve = _____

2   Gloomy = _____   5   Foolish = _____

(D) Can you write these words backwards and then place these new words into alphabetical order? [10]

| broom | coop | indoors | keen | loop |

_____   _____   _____   _____   _____

1st _____   2nd _____   3rd _____   4th _____   5th _____

(💡) **Helpful Hint**

With double vowels we mostly double the 'o' or the 'e'. Some words such as aardvark or skiing will have other doubled vowels but this is rare.

Unit 6

E All of these words are compound words. This means that they are made from two other words. Can you use a line to join up the two separate words that make up the compound word? [16]

snow	moon	pass	out	rain	out	over	pack
pass	rail	over	rain	snow	over	snow	out

flake	all	bow	word	age	heard

standing	law	light	side	ball

take	port	way	coat	drop

F Popular words for the first compound are prepositions, nature words, colours and body parts. The rest are 'odd bods' which can make up their own category. Can you divide your words into the following three columns? The first three words have been done for you as an example. [13]

PREPOSITIONS	NATURE	OTHER
Outlaw	Moonlight	Package

Moonlight

Outlaw

Outside

Outstanding

Overall

Overheard

Overtake

Package

Passport

Password

Railway

Rainbow

Raincoat

Snowball

Snowdrop

Snowflake

💡 **Helpful Hint**

Make sure that you know all of your prepositions as this will help you with compound word questions.

29

Argue

Build

Business

Definite

Desperate

Enough

Especially

Exercise

Guide

Particular

Peculiar

Perhaps

Possession

Separate

Special

Thought

20

Ⓖ All of the words in your list are tricky to spell and sometimes little rhymes or mnemonics can help us to remember how to spell them. Can you work out which word these spelling aids help with? [10]

1   There are four hissing snakes in this word.   _____

2   The <u>Bus</u> number <u>1</u> visits the Loch <u>Ness</u> monster.   _____

3   'I' 'C' 'U' in the middle of this word.   _____

4   **G**uide **us in d**ark **e**venings.   _____

5   There is 'a rat' in this word.   _____

6   **A r**ow **g**reatly **u**psets **e**veryone.   _____

7   'C' I'm before **ALL** in this word.   _____

8   Are 'U' a 'liar' at the end of this word?   _____

9   'th' symmetry around the letters OUG.   _____

10 Spell me backwards from tail to head,
    I know Every **TIN I FED**.   _____

Ⓗ Can you place some of your words into the grid below? [10]

Unit 7

(A) All of your words are in the grid, but the letters have been replaced with numbers. Can you work out which number represents each letter to solve the puzzle? [18]

A	B	D	E	G	H	I	K	L	M	N	O	P	R	S	T	U	W	X
												4						

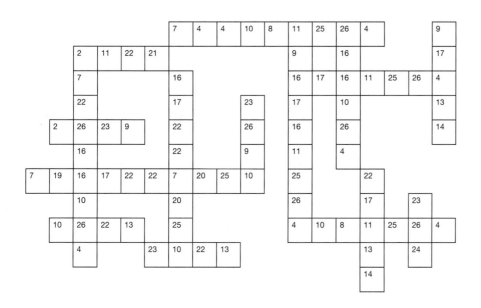

(B) A synonym is a word whose meaning is most similar to another word. Which of your words are synonyms for the following words? [4]

1 Vanish _____

3 Sunset _____

2 Sunrise _____

4 Unmanageable _____

Appear

Dawn

Disappear

Dusk

East

Impossible

Irregular

North

Popular

Possible

Regular

South

Unpopular

Wane

Wax

West

Helpful Hint

Sometimes an opposite word uses a prefix such as 'im', 'in', 'dis' or 'ir'. When you see words beginning like this, work out the root of the word and you will have more of an idea as to the meaning of the whole word.

22

Creepy

Flood

Freezing

Loose

Meeting

Moor

Needle

Noon

Queen

Sheet

Smooth

Spoon

Steep

Teeth

Weekend

Wooden

29

© All of the words in your list have been added to the grid but they are missing all of their letters except for the first one. Can you fill in the rest of the grid so that all of the words are in place? [16]

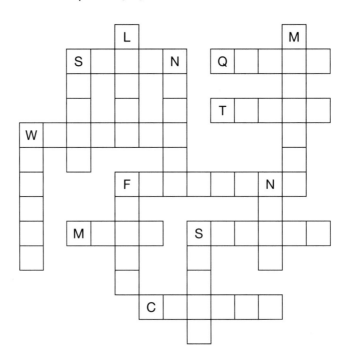

Ⓓ When we have double vowels it often changes the sound, for example two 'o's sound like 'oo'. Divide your words up into the right groups, the first example of each has been done for you. [13]

oo	E	Not oo or E
Noon	*Meeting*	*Flood*

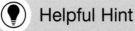 **Helpful Hint**

Always think about your sounds before spelling a word. If the sound is 'E' the word is likely to have a 'magic e' on the end OR double 'e' OR 'ea' in the word. Now try writing down a word using these three ways and see if this helps you.

(E) All of the words in your list are in the grid but only the first letters are here. Can you fill in the gaps so that the grid is complete? [16]

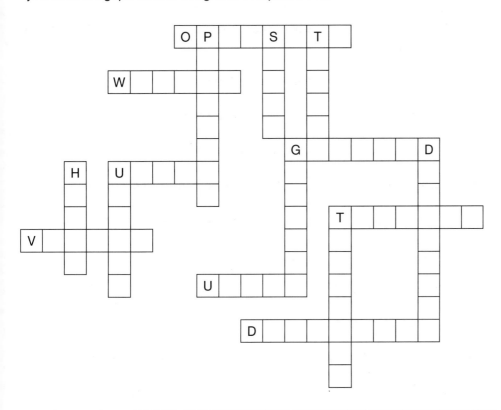

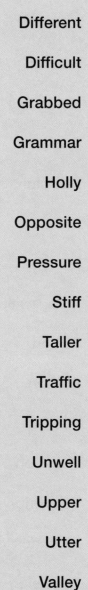

Different

Difficult

Grabbed

Grammar

Holly

Opposite

Pressure

Stiff

Taller

Traffic

Tripping

Unwell

Upper

Utter

Valley

Warren

(F) An antonym is a word most opposite in meaning to another word. Which of your words are antonyms for the following words? [4]

1 Easy   _____   3 Lower   _____

2 Released   _____   4 Shorter   _____

💡 Helpful Hint

When there are double consonants check whether it is a double letter BEFORE a suffix and if so, remember our spelling rule. If a word ends in a SINGLE consonant and the letter before is a SINGLE vowel, we double the last letter before adding our suffix. Following the rule will make the correct spelling most of the time.

20

Addition

Caution

Collection

Creation

Decision

Division

Mention

Multiplication

Option

Portion

Position

Question

Reduction

Rejection

Television

Version

16

(G) Add one of the words from your list into each space so that these sentences make sense: [16]

1   We save money because our school offers a _____ if we use their bookshop.

2   The pizza was divided so that we each had an equal _____ of it.

3   We had to make a _____ whether to buy a dog or a cat.

4   The baker's wedding cake was an amazing _____ .

5   Please don't _____ the secret party next weekend.

6   There was one _____ , but everyone else accepted our ideas.

7   Six plus two is an _____ sum.

8   Six times two is a _____ sum.

9   Six shared by two is a _____ sum.

10 We put the bird box in the best _____ ; out of rain, sun and wind.

11 After my homework I can watch the _____ for an hour.

12 Our library has a large _____ of local books.

13 We have the hard back _____ of that poetry book.

14 The pudding has the _____ of custard or cream.

15 _____ stops us running across the road without looking first.

16 The winner would be announced after the last _____ .

 Helpful Hint

'tion' or 'sion' endings are often tricky. If the root words ends in 't' we use 'tion' but if the root word ends in 's' or 'd' we use 'sion' but this rule can be broken.

Unit 8

Ⓐ All of the words in your list are here in the grid, with clues in the boxes. Can you use your words to complete the grid? [16]

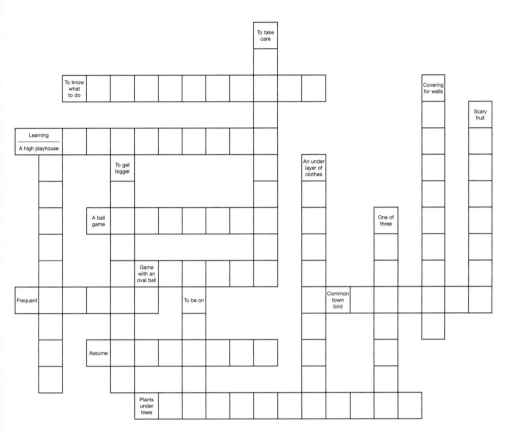

Carefully

Increase

Knowledge

Netball

Often

Pigeon

Pumpkin

Rugby

Suppose

Treehouse

Triplet

Undergrowth

Understand

Underwear

Upon

Wallpaper

Ⓑ Can you divide any six of your compound words into their two separate words? The first one has been done as an example. [6]

　　___In___ + ___Crease___ = ___Increase___

1 _____ + _____ = _____

2 _____ + _____ = _____

3 _____ + _____ = _____

4 _____ + _____ = _____

5 _____ + _____ = _____

6 _____ + _____ = _____

22

Unit 8

Brass

Cheese

Chess

Corridor

Giraffe

Glass

Guess

Knitting

Lettuce

Rabbit

Retell

Shrill

Skull

Sparrow

Stallion

Telling

(c) All of the words in your list are in the grid, but the letters have been replaced with numbers. Can you work out which number represents each letter to solve the puzzle? [18]

A		L	
B		N	
C		O	
D		P	
E		R	
F		S	
G		T	
H		U	
I		W	
K	22		

| 11 | 6 | 12 | 24 | 24 | | | | | | | | 25 |
| 16 | | | | | | | 14 | 2 | 12 | 12 | 24 | 12 |

(Grid puzzle with numbers: 24 13 17 25 25 4 8 2 — 23; 22 24 17 12 12; 6 24 5 25 17 24 24 16; 16 5 24 2 25 26 16 16; 16 26 12; 22 20 26 23 23 26 20 11 23; 12 23; 24 23 17 16 16 26 4 20 6; 16 14; 14 4 25 25 26 10 4 25 12; 20; 11 26 25 17 15 15 12)

(d) Can you place your words into the correct groups below? [15]

Double 'S': _Brass_ 1 _____ 2 _____ 3 _____

Double 'L': 4 _____ 5 _____ 6 _____ 7 _____ 8 _____

Double 'F': 9 _____

Double 'E': 10 _____

Double 'R': 11 _____ 12 _____

Double 'T': 13 _____ 14 _____

Double 'B': 15 _____

 Helpful Hint

Remember that the best way to consolidate your words is to use them in your writing whenever you can, so use, don't lose, your spelling skills!

33

Unit 8

E All of the words are hidden in the word search. Once you have found all of the words, the remaining letters spell out a message that is related to your words. [17]

1   What is this message? _____

B	A	D	M	I	N	T	O	N	T	E	N	N	I	S	G
A	A	M	R	O	U	N	D	E	R	S	R	E	S	A	C
S	W	I	M	M	I	N	G	N	S	Q	U	A	S	H	R
E	D	S	P	S	N	O	O	K	E	R	N	J	O	O	I
B	A	S	K	E	T	B	A	L	L	R	N	U	G	C	C
A	T	H	L	E	T	I	C	S	T	V	I	D	O	K	K
L	O	J	U	M	P	I	N	G	C	A	N	O	L	E	E
L	B	U	L	A	R	R	I	D	I	N	G	Y	F	Y	T

F Can you divide your words up into 'ball' games and 'no ball' games? [16]

Ball Games	No Ball Games

Athletics

Badminton

Baseball

Basketball

Cricket

Golf

Hockey

Judo

Jumping

Riding

Rounders

Running

Snooker

Squash

Swimming

Tennis

33

Camp

Cap

Clamp

Clap

Claps

Clasp

Lamp

Laps

Lump

Lumps

Palms

Saps

Slam

Slap

Slump

Spa

(G) An anagram is a word that can make another word if you rearrange the letters. All of the words in your list can be made out of the letters A, C, L, M, P, S, U. Using the pyramid, can you move between the letters spelling out all of your words? You can move vertically, horizontally and diagonally and forwards or backwards. [16]

						C						
					A	M	P					
				C	L	A	M	P				
			A	P	C	L	A	P	S			
		C	L	A	S	P	C	L	A	P		
	L	A	P	S	P	L	U	M	P	S	A	
P	A	L	M	S	A	P	S	L	U	M	P	S
L	A	M	P	S	L	A	P	S	L	A	M	S	P	A
				S	L	U	M	P				

(H) Can you find another 10 words that use any mix of the letters A, C, L, M, P, S, E, U? [10]

1 _____	6 _____
2 _____	7 _____
3 _____	8 _____
4 _____	9 _____
5 _____	10 _____

Unit 9

A Can you use the clues below to fill in the crossword? All of the words in your list fit in the grid as the answers. [16]

Across

2 A musical brass instrument
5 An arachnid
7 A wasp or bee attack
8 An item of clothing with buttons
9 An item of clothing
10 To slap or hit
11 They keep our hands warm

Down

1 Skin
2 To punch
3 The bottom of our face
4 Using a pen or pencil
6 Liquid food
7 Our backbone
8 To keep our neck warm
9 To push or barge
12 A long-necked bird

Chin

Drink

Flesh

Gloves

Scarf

Shirt

Shove

Skirt

Smack

Spider

Spine

Sting

Swan

Thump

Trumpet

Writing

 Helpful Hint

Always sound out your words if they are tricky to spell. Words like these have double consonants to begin the words. A word such as 'writing' is tricky because of the silent 'w' but other words can be sounded out and this can help.

16

Unit 9

Cause

Cheek

Curtain

Dairy

Diary

Diet

Fairy

Fiery

Flavour

Fruit

Goose

Lion

Mainly

Piano

Saint

Toast

B Using a line, join the correct word with its definition. [16]

1	Cause	A fabric covering for a window.
2	Cheek	Grilled bread.
3	Curtain	Milk, cheese, cream and yoghurt food types.
4	Dairy	Very hot.
5	Diary	A large bird.
6	Diet	A person who has lived an especially religious life.
7	Fairy	The opposite of 'effect'.
8	Fiery	Part of our face.
9	Flavour	A percussion musical instrument with a keyboard.
10	Fruit	A little book with days and dates in it.
11	Goose	A little mythical creature with wings.
12	Lion	Mostly.
13	Mainly	An animal that roars and lives in groups called 'prides'.
14	Piano	The food and drink that we eat.
15	Saint	The taste of something.
16	Toast	Apple, orange, pear and cherry food types.

16

 Helpful Hint

Double vowels have a spelling rule to help. Remember: *When two vowels go together walking, the first letter does the talking.* So 'ea' sounds like 'E' and 'ie' sounds like 'I' most of the time.

(C) All of the words are hidden in the word search. Once you have found all of the words, the remaining letters spell out a message that is related to your words. [17]

1 What is this message? _____

A	N	I	M	A	L	A	L	L	O	H	F
C	A	M	A	M	M	A	L	T	F	O	U
T	T	H	T	Y	P	I	C	A	L	S	N
U	U	P	E	E	S	E	W	O	O	P	N
A	R	E	R	C	A	N	A	L	R	I	A
L	A	T	I	R	D	S	E	N	A	T	T
D	L	A	A	M	E	T	A	L	L	A	U
W	I	L	L	T	G	L	O	B	A	L	R
F	E	S	T	I	V	A	L	H	A	L	A
C	A	S	U	A	L	A	N	N	U	A	L

(D) Can you add one of your words in each space so that these sentences make sense? [4]

1 There was a ladybird sitting on the flower's _____ .

2 Every February we have our _____ meeting.

3 Last summer we took a boating holiday to cruise the Shropshire _____ .

4 When I broke my leg I had an emergency x-ray at the local _____ .

Actual

Animal

Annual

Canal

Casual

Festival

Floral

Global

Hospital

Mammal

Material

Metal

Natural

Petal

Typical

Unnatural

(💡) Helpful Hint

Remember that words with an 'l' sound at the end can be spelt with 'le' (candle, angle), 'el' (gravel, angel) as well as 'al'. Sometimes writing down all three options can help you to recognise which ending is spelt correctly.

21

Unit 9

Brought

Count

Countries

Course

Curious

Famous

Fought

Group

Lounge

Ought

Pounce

Should

Trousers

Various

Would

Youngest

16

(E) Can you add one word from your list in each space so that these sentences make sense? [16]

1   Dad had a new pair of _____ for his birthday.

2   For the party I _____ the present and card with me.

3   I was _____ to find out what was in the other boxes.

4   My _____ child is only two years old.

5   I _____ to visit my aunt today as she is unwell.

6   There are _____ after-school clubs that we can join.

7   Greece, Poland and France are all _____ in Europe.

8   I cannot believe that he _____ break his leg just before the running race.

9   We waited in the hotel _____ until our taxi arrived.

10 We are doing a first aid _____ at school next week.

11 The little boy could now _____ up to ten.

12 They are a friendly _____ that were on our coach.

13 The two brothers _____ over the television remote control.

14 My friend has a _____ cousin who sings in a well-known band.

15 The cat tried to _____ on the mouse but missed and skidded into the wall.

16 We _____ take an umbrella in case it rains.

Ⓐ All the words in your list are in the grid but only the first letters are here. Can you fill in the gaps so that the grid is complete? [16]

Ⓑ If we take one letter from these words, what other words can be made? [4]

1	Amount	_____	**3**	Chant	_____
2	Burn	_____	**4**	Meant	_____

Ⓒ Can you write the following words backwards and then put these new words into alphabetical order? [10]

| recent | rodent | decent | content | distant |

_____ _____ _____ _____ _____

1st _____   **2nd** _____   **3rd** _____   **4th** _____   **5th** _____

Accident

Account

Amount

Burnt

Chant

Confident

Content

Decent

Disappoint

Distant

Experiment

Giant

Meant

Recent

Rodent

Spelt

30

Unit 10

Bacon

Certain

Chicken

Grain

Guardian

Onion

Potion

Robin

Salmon

Sudden

Urban

Wagon

Widen

Woken

Woman

Women

(D) Can you use the clues given to fill in the crossword? All of the answers are in your word list. [16]

Across

2 A vehicle
5 A female adult
6 To be definite
7 A spell
9 More than one female adult
10 Quick
13 A garden bird
14 A hen

Down

1 Cut of meat
3 Someone who looks after
4 A vegetable
5 Interrupted from sleep
8 A fish
9 To make broader
11 Not rural
12 Cereal

 Helpful Hint

All of these words end in 'n' which is the second-most used consonant in the whole alphabet. It can have every vowel, plus some consonants in front of it when it ends or begins a word and it often has a silent letter in front of it. Why not give yourself one minute to find as many words as you can that have 'n' as a starting letter, as an ending letter and as a middle letter in a word?

16

(E) All of the words in your list are in the grid, but the letters have been replaced with numbers. Can you work out which number represents which letter to solve the puzzle? [19]

A		N	
C		O	
D		P	
E		R	
F		S	
G	21	T	
I		U	
K		V	
L		W	
M		Z	

20	5	20	9	13

11	19	25	13

22

10

18

25	4	11	8	20	6	13

21	11	20	6	13

22		19		23

19

13		5		20

21

18		5

16	11	19	1	13

25	23	20	23	13

20		10		25

11

5		15		20	7	19	14	13

5		13		22		15

13		13		10

8

25	22	10	6	13

(F) Can you change these singular words into plurals? The first one has been done as an example for you. [8]

   Programme   *Programmes*

1 Rifle   _____

2 Rose   _____

3 Slice   _____

4 Surface   _____

5 Knife   _____

6 Vine   _____

7 Sale   _____

8 State   _____

Amaze

Awoke

Compare

Drove

Else

Grace

Knife

Programme

Rifle

Rose

Sale

Slice

State

Surface

Tame

Vine

27

Unit 10

Calendar

Cellar

Consider

Farmer

Finger

Guitar

Manager

Quartet

Remember

Similar

Sugar

Sweater

Teacher

Teenager

Unclear

Vicar

16

Ⓖ Can you draw a line to join the word to its correct definition? [16]

1	Calendar	Someone who gives an education to pupils.
2	Cellar	A group of four.
3	Consider	An organiser of months and dates.
4	Farmer	An underground storage room.
5	Finger	Someone who leads a church congregation.
6	Guitar	Someone between 13 and 19 years old.
7	Manager	To think about.
8	Quartet	Someone in charge.
9	Remember	A jumper.
10	Similar	Confused.
11	Sugar	Someone who looks after cows, pigs and sheep.
12	Sweater	A sweet additive.
13	Teacher	A stringed musical instrument.
14	Teenager	A digit on our hands.
15	Unclear	To be alike.
16	Vicar	To not forget.

Unit 1

Ⓐ **Left-over letters spell:** WORDS WITH EA

Ⓔ **Left-over letters spell:** THESE WORDS ALL USE TH OR CH

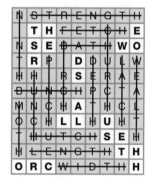

Unit 2

Ⓐ **Left-over letters spell:** WORDS THAT ARE FRUIT

Unit 3

Ⓕ **Left-over letters spell:** THESE ALL END IN A T

Unit 5

Ⓒ **Left-over letters spell:** COLOURFUL WORDS

Unit 8

Ⓔ **Left-over letters spell:** GAMES AND SPORT VOCABULARY

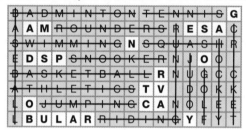

Ⓖ

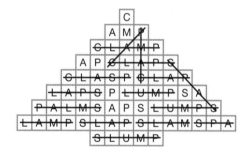

Unit 9

Ⓒ **Left-over letters spell:** ALL OF THESE WORDS END WITH AL

Progress Chart

How did you do? Fill in your score below and shade in the corresponding boxes
to compare your progress across the different tests and units.

50%	100%		50%	100%

Unit 1, p3 Score: __ / 25

Unit 6, p27 Score: __ / 15

Unit 1, p4 Score: __ / 26

Unit 6, p28 Score: __ / 19

Unit 1, p5 Score: __ / 24

Unit 6, p29 Score: __ / 29

Unit 1, p6 Score: __ / 22

Unit 6, p30 Score: __ / 20

Unit 2, p7 Score: __ / 27

Unit 7, p31 Score: __ / 22

Unit 2, p8 Score: __ / 16

Unit 7, p32 Score: __ / 29

Unit 2, p9 Score: __ / 24

Unit 7, p33 Score: __ / 20

Unit 2, p10 Score: __ / 28

Unit 7, p34 Score: __ / 16

Unit 3, p11 Score: __ / 24

Unit 8, p35 Score: __ / 22

Unit 3, p12 Score: __ / 16

Unit 8, p36 Score: __ / 33

Unit 3, p13 Score: __ / 24

Unit 8, p37 Score: __ / 33

Unit 3, p14 Score: __ / 23

Unit 8, p38 Score: __ / 26

Unit 4, p15 Score: __ / 16

Unit 9, p39 Score: __ / 16

Unit 4, p16 Score: __ / 16

Unit 9, p40 Score: __ / 16

Unit 4, p17 Score: __ / 30

Unit 9, p41 Score: __ / 21

Unit 4, p18 Score: __ / 20

Unit 9, p42 Score: __ / 16

Unit 5, p19 Score: __ / 16

Unit 10, p43 Score: __ / 30

Unit 5, p20 Score: __ / 27

Unit 10, p44 Score: __ / 16

Unit 5, p21 Score: __ / 16

Unit 10, p45 Score: __ / 27

Unit 5, p22 Score: __ / 16

Unit 10, p46 Score: __ / 16